The Psychology of Keeping the Sale

By Yaa Diaspora

and

Freedom Claudine Hunt

Published by

Power Women Press

The Psychology of Keeping the Sale

For informational purposes only

This work is derived from the original training video written, recorded, and published as
Freedom Claudine Hunt (Copyright © 2012)

ISBN: 978-1511519557

Published in the United States of America by Power Women Press.

Table Of Contents

Introduction

The Psychology of Keeping the Sale: How to End the Pattern of Clients Backing Out On You, Once and For All is a sales training book for people who know how to close sales and have good sales techniques, but have a large percentage of customers reneging or backing out.

This is a book about sales psychology and things you, as a salesperson, are largely unaware of that influence your ability to retain your sales.

If you aren't aware of how your customers make sales decisions or the counterproductive things you are saying and doing, you'll keep saying and doing them, and people will keep lying, avoiding you, agreeing then backing out, and wasting your time.

You'll want to pay close attention and take this information seriously because this book offers information that can fix this.

The Psychology of Keeping The Sale can help all types of salespeople and entrepreneurs: coaches, consultants, advisors, freelancers, and even business owners who are selling physical products.

One of my favorite teachers in internet marketing, Dan Kennedy, always says that when we receive business training and advice, we should not ask ourselves *if,* but *how* information applies to us in our own business, even if the example is from a different industry. What I have to share will help you no matter what industry you are in and no matter what you are selling. There is always a nugget you can grab that can help.

I urge you to customize this information for yourself and use it to propel yourself to your next level.

This information is based on independent study I did, as a result of losing sales that I thought I had successfully closed. I wanted to know what I was doing wrong to cause this, so I found out.

Through my research, I found out that there is actual science – psychology — that explains why people won't buy or they'll buy and then back out. It Is called buyer's remorse or reneging. The cause, in psychological terms, is "cognitive dissonance."

My psychology research, along with what I learned through being a certified money coach, along with my own experience as a salesperson and a consumer, led me to come up with the information here I'm sure you will find helpful.

In this book, you will learn:

- The number one reason you're not keeping your sales - from a psychological perspective - despite giving great service, having great testimonials, and being very good at what you do

- Why the most excited customers, the ones with whom you have the best conversations and the best rapport, seem to be the first ones to back out. You'll find out why that enthusiasm and excitement is not always a good thing.

- The five real reasons people won't buy or why they might buy and then back out of the sale

- The actual science behind five popular pieces of standard, marketing and sales advice, offered in the internet marketing and coaching industries. These are things you have probably heard before, but today, you're going to understand it in a completely different way, because you're going to understand it from a psychological perspective.

- The freebie that is killing your sales and what to do about it

- The nine things you are saying and doing that actually encourage or trigger people to buy and then return it or renege and back out of the sale altogether

- The new segment to add to your sales conversation that guards against clients having second thoughts. You might have already taken a training course on delivering free sessions, which includes scripts and other materials designed to help you close the sale, but today I am going to teach you about an aspect of the conversation that no one is teaching. It is not a part of the usual training, but after I introduce this to you, you will see exactly why you should add it to your sales strategy.

- The five new questions to start asking during your free sessions that influence prospective clients to be frank with you

- What you should do the moment you hear the potential client or customer say yes. By doing what I will teach, you exponentially reduce the chances of them backing out.

- And believe it or not, there is more!

About The Author

I will give you the short version of my bio, but first I must inform you that I am not a licensed psychologist or financial advisor. The information presented here is for informational purposes only and is not intended to treat, diagnose, or cure any psychological sales or money problems.

I am known by many names, depending upon which industry you met me in. I have been a full-time business owner since I left my corporate job in real estate in 2003 to become a full-time poet. That decision launched my publishing and speaking careers and taught me through trial and error, the ins and outs of making, marketing, and selling products and services.

In 2010, I was introduced to the coaching and internet marketing communities, and I became trained as a certified money coach, by one of the industry's most phenomenal, millionaire mentors, Kendall Summerhawk. I have coached in the areas of finding your purpose, building your business, writing and publishing, and attracting money. Now, I primarily work with power women and women in the spotlight on the many topics associated with their lifestyle, business, and status.

In addition to having earned a Bachelors degree in Behavioral Science with an Emphasis in Community Health, I am the principal consultant at Georgia Center for the Whole Businesswoman LLC. The organization deals with all areas that affect a professional or entrepreneurial woman's wellbeing, which covers areas outside of business, marketing, and sales.

In addition to doing the research that informs this book, my training and experience, along with being in the world as a consumer, have given me a holistic way of viewing marketing, sales, and sales retention.

On the next page, I share a few interesting statistics on my sales history. It is not a comprehensive picture, but it is designed to let you know who and what I am.

Business is my passion and I am grateful that you are sharing my passion with me right now, through reading my work.

A Few Interesting Sales Stats

- I once closed a paid teaching gig at a college before I even had a degree. I taught it for several semesters and received great student evaluation feedback (100%).

- I have a history of closing speaking engagements worth several thousand dollars, while colleagues say that the market will only bear a fraction of what I receive

- I have a near perfect closing rate of selling poetry-related products after performances, where colleagues complain that audience members never have money

- With the exception of ONE story (which now appears in a book alongside the work of the editor who rejected it where I received six times more than she was going to pay), I have a 100% closing rate on the traditional publication of all work written under my erotica pen name. This enables my work to be in bookstores around the world and for me to receive royalties that come in from different countries from the sale of my self-published work written under that name

- I once closed a sale worth several hundred dollars to teach a memoir-writing course that I made up on a whim while speaking to the book club at my local library

The Most Revealing Sales Statistic of Them All

The only time my sales suffered was when I was having confidence issues, due to letting cynical people influence me.

During this time, I had trouble focusing. I always tried to close sales in fear; I spent too much time trying impress the prospect instead of letting my natural light shine through, and I kept going from one project and "strategy" to another.

Each sales conversation was a replica of the last, until it made no sense to continue talking to prospects at all.

When I learned to control my confidence, I learned to control my cash flow.

Dedication

I wrote this because it hurts to see people who have wonderful gifts give up because they can't keep clients. Worse is when they become obsessed with a failed business experience from long ago. I call this "The Big Al Syndrome."

A former client of mine was once obsessed with a situation that occurred with a customer, who was known as Big Al. Big Al backed out of a sale, which caused a bunch of problems for my client and almost a decade later my client was still affected by it. Every time this client was in a sales situation, they would freeze up because of what happened with Big Al – finally deciding that there was no point in cultivating that business anymore. Big Al was such a huge part of this client's business identity that Big Al truly was "big". It was as if he was the god that held the keys to future revenue.

This obsession with failure didn't benefit my client and was heart-wrenching to hear about. I am happy to report that my client finally released the Big Al situation and went on to continue closing sales in that industry again.

I share my information with you so that you will never again be held back by your own Big Al. I dedicate this book to everyone who has sales trauma to release.

Human Nature and Sales

The first thing to be aware of when you're in a sales situation is that you're dealing with a human being, and human beings have a natural tendency to back out of potentially bad situations. It is human nature.

Now, you might say this isn't true. You might say that not everyone is like that. Well, the ability to access the safety of a situation and decide on whether or not we want to participate is part of what makes us human. To exempt a person from that and refuse to hold that understanding is to set yourself up for disappointment right from the beginning.

To reiterate – humans have a tendency to want to back out of potentially bad situations.

Managing that tendency in your prospects is the topic of this training.

The solution seems simple enough. You must convince the person you're selling to that this is not a bad situation. You can do that once you get past all of the natural defenses in his or her mind.

Sales Psychology 101

The following information will help you understand why people would want to back out of decisions that they make, even if they are positive decisions – specifically, the decision to buy from you.

Introducing Cognitive Dissonance

There is a term in psychology that explains it. The term is *cognitive dissonance*. Cognitive dissonance describes the conflict that happens within a person. It's about internal discord or disharmony. Cognitive dissonance explains why you might want to do one thing but you also want to do something else that seems contrary to that. We all have that. Some people call it an internal conflict. It's a mental and emotional conflict.

Introducing Cognitive Consonance

There is another term, *cognitive consonance*, that describes the opposite. Cognitive consonance means that you have harmony and consistency between what you say you want and what you do. Dissonance is when harmony is not there. As a salesperson you are dealing with dissonance all the time.

Joy and Pain

Another important principle to remember is that human beings are always looking to go towards pleasure and away from pain. If you have studied psychology, you have heard this before, but it is important to understand how this applies to making and keeping your sales.

Even though a person might want consonance (harmony), they might be willing to experience dissonance (disharmony, conflict, contradiction) in order to be "safe" and maintain a familiar feeling, which they might even interpret as pleasurable.

In sales, you're dealing with the fact that even though a person might have a problem that they recognize needs to be solved, they might not be willing to go through with the plan they made with you to solve their problem, because having a predictable routine and predictable outcomes is pleasurable, even if the "same ole same" produces negative results. In this case, changing what is predictable might cause some pain, which is undesirable.

Beware the Overly Excited Prospect

It is not unusual for you to find someone that needs your services so badly that they are extremely excited to talk with you about buying. Unfortunately, these overly excited people tend to be the ones who back out the quickest.

It seems strange that these people would bail out on you faster than those who are reluctant, but my research reveals why this makes perfect sense, and can even be expected.

Remember what I explained about consonance and dissonance. There are two sides at play when a decision is made, so when a person comes to you overly excited, they are only identifying with one side of the mental process; one half of what's going on inside of them. Inevitably, the other side, disharmony, will show its face. That is when you'll receive the email or call that they are backing out. Or you won't hear anything from them anymore and they become a totally different person, ducking, dodging, and ignoring you.

When a person comes to you excited, they're not thinking about the part of them that will pull out later on that night when they remember their electric bill is too high and they're trying to cut back on expenses, or when they tell their significant other they authorized a purchase and their significant other doesn't see why they need it. However, just because they're not thinking about these things while they're talking to you, doesn't mean you should be fooled into thinking it'll never come up.

You want it to come up while you're on the phone with them so that you can address it.

When they're overly excited, you can know for sure that they're not acknowledging both sides of the psyche – the side that says "Yes, this is great and we're looking forward to it" and the side that says "No, we don't!"

See, those prospects that interrogate you with a million questions, even trick questions, are showing you their cognitive dissonance and giving you a chance to influence it. This is great because it won't sneak up on either of you. On the other hand, the prospects who are overly excited don't even acknowledge their fears. This makes the fears so much more powerful when they show up, especially since you won't be there to address them. But do you know who *will* be there? I'll tell you: those friends and family members who stand in alignment with the fears and are telling the potential client every reason why they shouldn't trust you, why they shouldn't buy, why they can do it themselves, get it for free, wait another few months, etc. Those who resonate with the fear will be in close proximity, so it is best for you and the prospect to address the dissonance before it shows up on its own.

Discussing the client's fears about buying is vital to making and keeping the sale. Too many salespeople are trying to avoid reasons why someone wouldn't buy and hoping it won't come up. This is the wrong approach.

"But I Thought They Really Liked Me!"

You would not believe the amount of people who tell me that they end up feeling surprised or hurt after their sales conversations, because they believed the prospect who backed out had liked them. Please understand that a prospect's decision to back out is not a result of suddenly not liking you. They are backing out for other reasons, having to do with their unaddressed inner conflicts. Sometimes the conflict is about what they want to accomplish versus what it is going to take to accomplish it. Other times it is about the changes that can occur that they aren't ready for or experiencing secondary results they didn't intend on. Again, they are afraid of these consequences even though they are results of positive change.

They're not backing out because they don't like you and I know it might sound crazy, but they're not buying just because they like you, either. Of course, liking you helps facilitate the sale, but they are also buying because they know you can help them solve their problem and because you addressed all the reasons they would renege.

That means, the reason you're not keeping your sales, despite your great service, your testimonials, and your superior skill is because you are only concentrating on the reasons why they *should* buy, and you have completely bypassed or not sufficiently addressed the reasons why they *shouldn't* or the reasons they might have for backing out.

To be clear, I'm not saying that you should give potential clients a list of reasons not to buy. I am saying that you should address the fears and objections you know exist, even if they are not thinking about it right now.

You must be on alert, because *you know* how this goes. There is no benefit to tip-toeing around what you've seen happen over and over again, so be bold and creative in confronting it.

The Pain of Not Buying

In addition to exploring reasons they might not buy, you should also discuss the pain, inconvenience, and problems that persist if they decide not to buy. The prospect has to leave the conversation feeling like no matter what it takes to buy, and what other situations come up, it is better than staying in their current condition.

Dissonance Theory and Internal Conflict in Sales

I would like you to understand dissonance theory and internal conflict a little more.

In my opinion, the most significant thing about dissonance theory is that people truly want consonance (harmony) and do not want dissonance (discord), so even the craziest things you see, hear, and experience in business reflect your clients' attempts at gaining harmony. They can go to extreme lengths to justify their contradictory decisions and you must not take it personally.

There are three aspects of dissonance theory that you're dealing with at all times in sales. They are:

1) dissonance (being inconsistent or contrary)

2) consonance (being in harmony)

3) irrelevance (things that have no bearing on the topic at hand)

In other words, your prospective customer is either going to be:

1) In alignment with making the purchase

2) Reluctant to make the purchase

3) Taking time to consider things that don't have any impact on the sale or the results they receive from making the purchase

You need to know which of these three aspects are at play with your customer, in order to facilitate and keep the sale.

Things That Influence Dissonance

It is also important to know the two main things that influence dissonance, so that you can understand more about what's going on inside your potential customer or client's mind.

One thing that influences the dissonance is the amount of mental and emotional unease going on inside them. If they are highly stressed or agitated, it will negatively impact their ability to make a decision and stick with it. This is useful information for those who sell life coaching and other products to people who are having a difficult time in their lives. Theoretically, the more difficulty they are having, the harder it will be for them to step out of it, by getting the help, because it requires them to step out of acting upon their self-defeating beliefs. For you, that means that it could be harder to close and keep the sale.

The other thing that influences dissonance is the *importance* of the thoughts and feelings they are having, because not all thoughts carry equal weight.

On one hand, we are talking about just how much *stuff* a person is dealing with that would cause them to say one thing and do another. On the other hand, we are talking about the importance of the beliefs and thoughts they have—how strongly they hold onto them.

Some beliefs are stronger than others, and at any given time, you are dealing not only with a prospect's quantity of beliefs, but the quality of them too. It is their beliefs that will help them decide to buy and honor the transaction, or to decide to buy and then back out. (Or not buy at all.)

Common Attempts to Justify Inconsistency

Typically, there are three things people do to try to reduce their dissonance to make themselves feel better about the incongruent decision they are making. (i.e. decision to buy and back out)

1. They lower the importance of the dissonant factor. In plain language, this means they'll say that the contradiction is not a big deal. They might say that everyone has contradictions and take an attitude of, "So what?"

2. They add consonant elements. In plain language, this means that they'll tell themselves what good things could happen for them as a result of *not* buying, *not* sticking with the sale, and *not* getting the help. This is sometimes done by suddenly adding on requirements for buying from you, such as demanding it at a certain price or at a certain time, even after the fact, all in an attempt to be able to state that backing out was good because the price or timing was a problem they are glad they avoided.

3. They change a dissonant fact. In plain language, this means that now they believe that the problem they have is not a bad thing at all and that it was a judgment error on their part to even consider it a problem.

Understanding this aspect of the way people think; the way they rationalize and make justifications, helps you see that it is not personal, it's not that you need to lower your fees, or do the other things they suddenly came up with to satisfy them (because those objections are not real). And it's not that they don't have a problem that requires your help. When they are experiencing inner turmoil and not dealing with it, making up these stories convinces them that it is okay for them not to get your help. Here's the thing: You must not let their stories convince you too!

How Society Condones Flighty Sales Behavior

Though it might be controversial, I believe that society condones dissonance and incongruent sales behavior, and aids it in two ways.

Buyer's Remorse Laws

Number one there are buyer's remorse laws. This is when consumers are given a few days, weeks, or months (depending upon what they are buying and which state the transaction took place in) to go back on their decision, after making a large purchase. Buyers are given what's called a *cooling off period* to go home and think about the purchase they made and return it if they want. The conditions of being able to make the return and get their money back varies. Sometimes they might have to pay a fee for the option to back out, or they might lose a percentage of what they paid. It's also possible that there are other contractual terms. Either way, the fact that there are buyer's remorse laws lets you know that dissonance is common and it is something we are in such deep acceptance of that we accommodate it. I'd rather see people be sure about the decision they make first, than to always have an out, because in my opinion, this culture of always having an out is why we see so many people backing out of commitments in other areas of their lives. It affects other people and is out of integrity. But that's another conversation.

I'm sure that what I'm saying can be controversial, however please don't confuse how I feel about the buyer's remorse laws with how I feel about return policies or money back guarantees, when something is wrong with the product. If something is wrong with a product, you should be able to get your money back. My problem is with the culture that says that we don't need to properly think through our decisions and stick to them, because we can always turn back. In fact, it is law.

I have seen people literally bank on this and profit from it. On the flip side, we're encouraged to create urgency with the customer so they can buy right away, without time to think about it. How does that line up with what I've just said?

When Customers Need to "Think About It"

Let me be frank. Most prospective customers who tell you they have to think about it are lying. They're just making an excuse to get away from you. They will not be thinking about anything having to do with you, your product, or your service once they escape from you.

My advice is if you know they really want or need the product or service and you know that there truly is a conflict going on inside them, then attempt to coach them to a decision instead of supporting their decision to "think". It is fine if the decision is no. Everything is not for everybody. If the decision is yes, that is wonderful. You will be glad to have helped them give themselves the gift of your product or service. But know the difference between who is worth the time investment of helping with their dissonance and whom you should leave alone. The ones, whom you know are just blowing you off, let them go somewhere far away and "think about it". You want customers who will be committed and whom you don't have to force anything on, so that you can make your sales guarantees with little to no worry of being taken advantage of, because your customers are in alignment with the purchase.

To reiterate, the "thinking" process is really a decision-making process, and it is fine to help the prospective client out with it.

A Woman's Prerogative

The second way I believe society caters to dissonance and incongruent sales behavior is the notion of "a woman's prerogative." While it is a woman's prerogative to change her mind (especially in sexual situations so please don't misquote or misunderstand me here), I have found that in sales, a lot of the woman's prerogative language condones being flighty, not thinking through decisions properly, and not making sure there is a full understanding of the benefits and drawbacks, under the justification of being able to back out later, because that's what a woman should be able to do. Then, as women, we become angry, when people see us as erratic and indecisive.

From what I have learned, that is not what womanhood is about. While changing your mind is a wonderful thing when you discover that, even after gathering and processing information, you made a decision that was not truly in your best interest, "a woman's prerogative" is harmful when the woman is changing a decision that is good for her into one that is bad for her; when she is exchanging a decision she made out of strength for a decision made out of fear. This does not help her advance even though it is her prerogative to do so. In that case, what good is prerogative?

But I digress.

As I stated before, being erratic and indecisive in one area of life usually shows up in another area of our lives too and negatively affects other people. This is not something related to gender, but we make it so when we call this type of behavior "a woman's prerogative."

The Five Real Reasons People Won't Buy OR Will Definitely Back Out, That You Can Do Something About

Let us discuss *the five real reasons* people won't buy, will make a promise to buy and then stand you up, or will buy and then back out. In essence, these are different manifestations of dissonance. I will tell you how to handle each of the five.

1. They are not sure that what you're selling is actually going to help them. This is different from the people who are afraid of success and are backing out because they <u>will</u> be helped. This is about the people who don't want to lose their money on a bad product or service. It is also about a prospect not unequivocally knowing whether or not you can help them. These are legitimate concerns, not minor insecurities.

You must have proof of your results from satisfied customers and a powerful guarantee to overcome this insecurity. There are different types of guarantees and different *aspects* you can guarantee, so don't worry if you are in an industry where a guarantee is inappropriate or illegal. Be creative with the assurances you offer.

2. They are not sure you have the skills, technology, or time to deliver what you said you would. This is a trust issue and in some cases, it is a "boundaries" issue, when people who know you're in demand are making judgments about what you can get done. Because we are accustomed to seeing people being overcommitted in their schedules, exaggerating their skills, underplaying their weaknesses, and not following through on their word – especially if the prospect is that type of person – they will believe you are like that too.

The key here is to *unquestionably* assure them of your credentials, experience, process, and accessibility, so that their uncertainty goes away.

3. They are uncomfortable with the time investment. Many people are strapped for time. They feel like they hardly have time to do what's already on their schedule, so they might view it as an imposition to try to cram something else into their schedule.

Here, you must help them change the dialogue from "cramming" to "allowing space for" and you must prove that this *investment* of time brings *returns* that those who are not willing to invest the time will never have access to. You must illustrate that the time

investment is the most significant aspect of gaining success in the area they seek improvement in.

4. They're uncomfortable with the financial investment. Not having enough money is such a common reason why people don't move forward with plans that people actually believe it has to be that way. A person with a fixed budget might say they don't have enough money before they even know how much something costs, even though you might be offering them extra time to pay for it, or another significant detail that would make it affordable. A person in this position might even volunteer details about their other financial obligations or state that they have other purchases in the works. These *are* important considerations.

This requires you to be sure this person fits your target market of people who can and do purchase from you; then show them examples of how people like them made it work. Your credentials, testimonials, letters of recommendation, and guarantee work well here, as does the investment conversation. Overall, you must convey that they are not the first to be in their situation and they won't be the last, but that they *can* make a positive change in their circumstances by figuring this out with you right now.

5. There's nothing in writing. When something is in writing it is real. It's contractual. Even though oral statements can be binding, when it's written, it's official. Prospects can see what they are getting and there is clarity that comes along with having a written document. Without that clarity and reassurance some people won't want to buy, or they'll back out because they're not really sure about what they just purchased.

The fix here is simple. In addition to having the contract, you should have a web page, brochure, one-sheet, or other type of written material that prospects can review that clearly explains all of the points discussed in the 5 reasons you just read about. This document covers all your bases so you should not be without it.

I'm going to give you a *bonus reason*. There can be many reasons, but I didn't want to overlook this one.

Bonus Reason: They are afraid there might be a better deal they're missing out on somewhere else.

Of course, as a respected expert, your preference is to stay away from customers and clients, who price shop, so that the value of what you have is more important to them than the cost of getting it. Until you reach that point, though, there will be people in your circle who know they want the product or service, believe in it, believe in you, have the time and money, and all...but they wonder if they can get a better deal from another company. Or they wonder if they wait a week if it'll go on sale.

Even if you feel insulted, address this issue by letting them know the one-of-a-kind nature of getting it from you and your company that they can't find anywhere else. Tell them what other perks they get from establishing a business relationship with you. This is an instance where you can benefit from knowing that some customers feel incentivized with bonuses that are outside of the actual product or service you are selling. It can be a tipping point for them. They sometimes want the extras more than the main offer. So go ahead and flaunt those extras that they can't get anywhere else. This will influence them to want to stick with you.

The Psychology Behind Your Guru's Famous Sales Advice

Even though I've already given you tips and advice on how to manage five (well, six) of the reasons clients don't buy or are prone to backing out, I'm going to go into the science behind five popular pieces of marketing and sales advice given in the coaching, internet marketing, and personal development industry, that come straight out of findings in psychology.

If you've ever been part of a coaching program, you will find that there are some common action steps your coaches and gurus will tell you take, but you do them half-heartedly, or not at all, and you don't get good results. Hopefully, by understanding the actual science behind the advice, you will be inclined to follow it and get better results. The following is a brief explanation of their suggestions.

1. Benefit from social proof. The most common element of social proof is testimonials or case studies, which are statements from people who have already bought from you, or people you worked with, who can attest to the results that you've produced for them and the way you treated them in business. For maximum effect, the statement should not simply state that you helped them. Instead, it should briefly detail how you helped *change their life for the better*. They should speak briefly about their situation before they came to you and the improvements they experienced as a result of coming to you. This statement should appear alongside the person's full name and photo, and should include a link to their website, social media page, or other proof that they are real person, whom you really helped.

This advice is based in psychology because it manages dissonance and discord. Just in case the prospect thinks you're exaggerating your claims, the testimonials demonstrate that other people have been helped by you and that you're the real deal. Even if they don't consciously like to follow the crowd, psychologically we feel better with other people's recommendations and endorsements, and are likely to follow their lead if the story is inspirational enough.

If a person has any rationality at all, they will have to accept the word of the people who have been helped. This is why online star ratings and book reviews are so popular. They are influential. Use this to your advantage. Social proof overrides the part of your prospect that is trying to pull away, out of fear, and puts them in harmony with their highest good, which is getting your product or service.

2. Sell the benefits not the features. For example, if you own a computer, you're not going to emphasize the point that it has a keyboard (which is a feature). Rather, you're going to discuss all the things you can do with the computer (which are benefits). People don't buy computers because they need keyboards – at least this is not the direct motivation. If they are entrepreneurs, they buy computers because computers allow them to accomplish business goals. You sell an entrepreneur a computer by emphasizing how it will help them make money. You sell an author a computer by emphasizing its word processing function, which allows them to easily write books and add more income and credibility to their brand. You sell a student a computer by stating that it allows them to easily access the information and tools they need to complete their college degree and land their dream job, and have a bright future. In all cases, you emphasize the built-in technology that helps avoid viruses, freezing, crashing, and other glitches that slow them down, waste their time, lose their work, and are overall major annoyances. There are people, whom you sell a computer to by stating how fast the processor is because it gives them the greatest experience playing their favorite online games. You must emphasize whatever the prospect gets *from the use of* the computer (or whatever they are buying from you), not just the technical things it is made of or that comes with it. That is the difference between features and benefits.

The psychology behind this is that speaking of benefits brings a person towards consonance and harmony, because it allows them to be able to agree to the idea of getting pleasure from utilizing what you are offering. They can picture themselves enjoying it and receiving results. On the other hand, speaking primarily of features encourages them to make a decision based on mundane, technical information, which does not do much to inspire them to spend the money with you, over a competitor, and could potential have them miss out on all that they can gain by buying from you. You don't want them to purchase, then get home and see it somewhere else cheaper, which we discussed earlier, and return it because you only sold them on technical specifications. Explaining benefits means it's no longer about price. Explaining benefits of working with *you* means there is no worthy competition.

3. Discover the pain and sell the pleasure. I have tried to drive home the point that humans move toward pleasure and away from pain, except when the road to pleasure could be painful. (Deep!). So you want to uncover what is causing the most pain in their lives so that you can sell them some relief. Promising pleasure over pain and being able to prove that you can follow through will earn you sales. Even if there's no apparent pain, you can promise *more pleasure*. The principle here is that pleasure is difficult for the human mind to resist. As a salesperson, you will profit if you remember this.

4. Offer a guarantee. Having a money back guarantee battles dissonance by stopping the prospect's urge to run away from you, due to believing they might end up losing something through working with you.

As I stated at the outset, human beings are prone to backing out. It is a built-in tendency; a protective mechanism. A guarantee says, "You don't have to run, it's okay; you can stay!" It gives them recourse against something bad happening. Money back guarantees are powerful in gaining trust and deserve some consideration.

I've already discussed my thoughts on buyer's remorse laws vs. money back guarantees, so I advocate being very deliberate about your guarantee. If you're in an industry where you are not supposed to give guarantees, you must be creative.

One of my mentors said that you can always guarantee *something*. Even if it is as simple as "I will respond within 48 hours." That can mean a lot to a person who feels unappreciated or unheard, or is paying a premium for access to you. Of course, there would have to be boundaries set around it so that they don't abuse the privilege. The point is you can find a guarantee if you are creative enough, even if the guarantee is not about money. A guarantee is psychologically reassuring and opens the door for them to make a decision to work with you and to stick with it.

5. Use a letter of agreement or contract with clear parameters. I cannot tell you the amount of times I have been screwed as a seller and a consumer due to not having a contract. These incidents stopped happening when I implemented a firm boundary of consistently using contracts.

Having a contract is instrumental in avoiding misunderstandings. While I'm not oblivious to the adage that a contract is only as good as the person who signs it (which means a dishonest person won't honor the contract even though they signed it), I've found the use of contracts to be a useful protocol. For the customer, it encourages consonance for several reasons. First, it documents that the payment is not forever. Although the client should already know that, seeing it written goes a long way toward letting them know there won't be any "funny business." Contractual payment terms reassure them that the financial agreement is finite, not infinite. There is a beginning and an end to it. This is much easier to stick with than something that is potentially ongoing, with no clear parameters. The written agreement also gives boundaries around the professional relationship and lets them know how things will be handled. This gives them a sense of security, which renowned psychologist, Abraham Maslow, stated in his Hierarchy of Needs pyramid, as the greatest human need outside of the physiological needs that keep us alive.

With so many things changing, this gives them a sense of what will become normal and that everything will be okay. This security appeals to the part of the psyche that will not commit, or at least not for long, by reminding them that this is only for a period of time. Having the information spelled out and signed appeals to the fearful part of them that needs to know every detail to feel secure. There is nothing wrong with that, especially when money is being exchanged. While you can't account for everything that will happen, because some arbitrary things come up as part of life, being able to inform prospects of the basic structure of the interaction helps them decide to make the purchase and stick with it. At the end of the day, the agreement helps them feel comfortable with everything, which is a psychological benefit. As the salesperson, you benefit from them feeling comfortable too. Last but not least, using written agreements is just good business.

How To Do "Free" Correctly

Coaches and consultants in internet marketing are taught that they should give something away as lead generation and as a sample in order to get sales.

I agree. It works in all industries.

"Free" is designed to help customers decide to buy from you. That is why promotions like "free shipping" work so well.

However, there is a type of freebie that kills your sales and I've seen many newbies sabotage themselves with it.

The Freebie That Is Killing Your Sales

The freebie that kills your sales is the one that makes the potential client feel like they've already hired you and therefore don't need to buy anything from you.

This is doesn't serve you or your market. You might think you're helping by doing this, but in most cases, you're not. If you've been in business long, or if you're prolific with your content, you might have several freebies out there that go so deep into your topic it defeats its sales generating purpose.

The freebie is designed to get a person started and display your expertise. It is not designed to have a person use it to completely solve their problem, especially if the problem is one that is better addressed with guidance from a skilled advisor such as you. It is unethical to give them so much information and position it as if they can use that material as a complete solution, when in reality, the complete solution involves working with you or using information that is contained in the full version of what you are selling, not the free sample. By all means, give them something comprehensive, but make certain they understand that this is not all there is. There's more.

Take this book for example. Even though it isn't free (it's low cost), salespeople can use my information to drastically improve their sales, but would need to talk to me for a complete overhaul of their sales closing process.

In this book, I'm telling you the psychological things going on in the mind of the prospect that can hinder the sale, but in working with me, we work through what is going on inside of *you* that hinders the sale, in addition to coming up with the strategies you're apt to be consistent with to make and keep sales.

As much as I hope you find value and are able to use the information in this book to stop losing sales, this book is limited to this topic. It is not personalized and does not address your particular story or situation. You'd have to speak with me to get insight and direction on your specific case and I make it known that, that is the outcome I prefer.

The Compliment That Is Not a Compliment

When your free information is great, but you allow a potential customer to believe that it is a complete solution, you hear things like, "I love you and your work! You are so amazing! I might want to get coaching from you someday but right now I just want to use your free stuff!"

It is as if your paid service is a distant option because they're planning to get the answers *from you* a different way.

Fix this by making sure:

a) Your freebie is in exchange for a way to contact them

b) Your freebie is highly targeted to the people most willing and able to buy

c) Your freebie stays on one particular topic

d) Your freebie gets people started on solving a problem

e) You offer a *compelling reason* and *easy opportunity* to get the full product

Now, there might be a step you offer before offering the full product, but you must offer something that gives you a chance to close a bigger sale. It might be an offer to speak with you, or a link to special pricing for a limited time, or another way to go deeper into the topic with them. No matter what, keep your ego in check and don't take it as a compliment that a person wants to use your free stuff to solve their problem (if you're in business). Besides, a phrase I've heard many times in business is that "people value what they pay for and pay for what they value". To utilize this principle, even your free stuff must lead to something that people can pay for and receive deeper value from.

About Your Free Sessions

While we're on the topic of free things, let's talk about your free session. Doing this research on psychology and sales has brought to light the depth of people's hidden motives and has led me to several insights or "aha moments." The insight I would like to share regarding the free session is especially important if you have ever had problems closing interested clients in your free sessions.

Here it is:

Some people see *talking* as an *action* step so they make it a goal to *talk* to you. They put it on their "to do" list to *talk* to a coach or consultant and check out whatever it is you do. The problem with this is people with this "goal" of "talking" get satisfaction the moment contact is made, because their hidden motive is to *talk*, not to buy, so that they can say they *talked* to someone. They get to check off something on their list from *attending* your free session, rather than by *signing up and doing the work*.

This is a subconscious thing, meaning it happens below the surface of their awareness. People don't realize they have this hidden motive. So the longer you stay on the phone with them during the session, the more satisfaction they get. The longer you stay on the phone coaching them, the more of the experience of having a coach without needing to buy, you're giving them. Then if you actually solve their problem on the call (solving it doesn't really happen in one call, but it can *feel* like the problem is solved when you've addressed a major aspect of the problem) you are short-changing them. This is because, as a coach or consultant, you know that even if you solve one aspect of a problem, more issues are going to come up, because there are usually a series of issues that manifest as "the problem", not just one issue. As the specialist, you probably deal with your client's issues in a particular order. You have a process. But if the person feels that everything is fixed because they talked to you in a free session, they won't have the opportunity to go through the process and get the entire problem, including the root of it, fixed.

As the expert, you are aware of what they are not aware of, but with getting too much out of the free session, they get satisfied and mark the "coaching experience" off of their list. They might even start referring to you as their mentor, advisor, or coach to people they want to impress, without having earned the right to call you that or invested in this type of relationship with you.

Solve this by following the guidelines you have been given on doing free sessions, especially the boundaries around time limits. If you haven't studied how to do your free sessions, this is something I can help you with if we decide to work together.

The New Segment to Add to Your Sales Conversation That Guards Against Second Thoughts

There is a new segment to add to your free session, which again is really a sales conversation and not a free coaching session unless you are coaching them into making a definitive decision about whether or not to go through with investing in your services. This is because being in limbo, without a definitive yes or no is not good for either of you. While you might really want to book this client, it is fine if they decide not to work with you. If that is the case, you want to know that instead of wasting time and energy on someone who is truly not interested. They should appreciate that too.

The following advice is something no one but me is teaching (as of this printing), but I've found that if you want to make your sales stick, you should add a section to your sales conversation about buyer's remorse. Of course, you won't call it that, but it's the segment where you make the person you're speaking with aware of dissonance so that it doesn't sneak up on them and they can be prepared for it when it comes and tries to spoil the progress, because it *does* come. If you address it before it happens you're going to seem like a genius *and* save the sale.

Discussing Dissonance With Your Customer

Tell them what dissonance looks and feels like and that it manifests by trying to talk them out of a positive decision. Say something like, "I know you're interested in this and I look forward to working with you. I just want to warn you that there's something that tends to comes up in us humans when we make a decision to improve our lives and I don't want it to ruin the progress we've made. Can I discuss it with you?"

The aim is to be brief as possible about this so that you can move on to closing the sale and processing the payment, but you still want to be thorough about it too. In a nutshell, tell them to expect the following things, designed to make them change their plans, but not to fall into that trap:

- *Thinking about what you're losing instead of what you're gaining* through the work that you're going to be doing. This can be time, money, or anything else that might have to be adjusted after you make a decision to move forward in your life.

- *Letting people talk you out of the decision that you made* that you know is right for you. This shows up in a lot of different ways, especially when people around you are not making positive changes in their own lives.

There's something that holds them back, so it is difficult for them to understand your decision to make changes despite having to give up, trade, or change something in order to facilitate the change.

- *Pushing deadlines to begin the work further down the line* or further away from when you know when you need it, which is now. This is a form of procrastination or putting it off altogether. What happens is, pushing it away a few weeks turns into a few months, which turns into a bunch of other things coming up, and before you know it, getting the help is not something you feel strongly about anymore and you don't do it.

- *Forgetting the plans you made to make the money needed to get the service* or saying those plans are not going to work. If money is an issue, you must stick to the plan for getting it and not succumb to lack of confidence or other issues that make it look like you're not going to be able to get the money. These are tests of your resolve and you have to push past them and show that you are in control and you *will* get the money.

Five Questions That Cut Through The B.S.

Let's move onto the five new questions you must start asking in your free sessions in order to distinguish the serious shoppers from the "talkers" and solidify your sales. These are questions that came to me as a result of immersing myself in this topic, studying, coaching, training, and even being a consumer. The answers to these questions provide powerful insight for you and the prospect.

Question 1: Have you really allowed yourself to buy?

Sometimes we want something but have not given ourselves permission to invest in it, which causes a conflict. We must be clear that if we want something we are 100% fine with buying it.

Question 2: What would it take for you to buy (today)?

They must know exactly what their criteria is and exactly what would satisfy them. If they know their criteria and it has been met, and they have given themselves permission to buy, then there's no reason *not* to buy. The only question might be one of how to do the transaction or payment arrangements if applicable, which can always be worked out.

Question 3: Is there someone else whose approval you'll need, or who can stop you from moving forward with this plan?

Most of the time, bringing up "the spouse objection" (where they say they have to talk to their spouse first and get back to you) is fake. It is a way to get out of making a firm decision. Sometimes, it can be real though. For example, I'm married and I'm not going to want to do something that my husband wouldn't be happy with. At the same time, I know that my husband is not going to stop me from doing something that's really good for me, because chances are it will be really good for *us*.

Everyone does not have this type of understanding in their relationship though. So if the answer is yes, there is someone who can stop them from doing what they want or need to do to improve their lives, a deeper question you're probably not going to want to get into (because it is actual coaching) is "How do you move forward if you're with someone who is unsupportive of the changes that you want to make in your life?" Though you won't ask this, you must be aware of the magnitude of this predicament so that you can proceed appropriately.

What you offer in this situation is the opportunity for the three of you to speak together about buying the item, or to include the spouse in the coaching or consulting package, so that both spouses receive value from what you are selling.

Sometimes this works. Other times you might have to let the sale go, because the prospective client might not be at a place where they can make independent decisions and it will ultimately be a problem for everyone if they go behind their spouse's back to buy from you.

Nonetheless, when you ask these questions you get to know who you're dealing with and what types of hidden issues are influencing the transaction.

Question 4: Does your partner/spouse know how this can be beneficial to them too?

Any improvement that your potential client makes as a result of the purchase is going to impact the relationship and/or household. So if they're hiring you because you can help them make more sales, get more clients, or have more peace of mind, or whatever it is your specialty is, chances are that thing is going to benefit the spouse as well. It could be as simple as realizing that now they have an expert they can turn to with questions, via their spouse. I've given plenty of mini-coaching sessions to spouses who needed a quick tip on something, even though the main client was their spouse. They were grateful to have an expert at hand. That is something to be considered and to make sure prospects are aware of.

Question 5: What do you allow yourself to buy that does not help the situation or actually wastes money?

Remember, these questions are being asked during the free session, which is a private, rapport-building conversation that consists of asking questions. The questions in this section are not your first questions – by the time you get to these questions, you have built rapport with previous questions – and when done correctly, there is no problem getting an honest answer to these questions.

This book assumes you already know how to conduct a free session, but for those who don't, I will share that it consists of you coaching them to gain clarity on the problem, on what they want, on what is stopping them from getting it, and on how they can begin to get it.

Understanding how to conduct your free session is vital to being able to ask revealing questions such as this one, but when you ask it, it helps the person see that they spend money on things that don't help, so they might as well spend money on something that actually does help.

Confidence On Behalf Of Your Potential Client

Help bring your prospects into consonance with the power of your beliefs. *You* hold the belief that their life can improve. *You* hold firm to the possibility, even if they can't hold the possibility for themselves. You are strong for them. You are strong *with* them, which encourages them to be brave enough to invest in working with you to manifest great possibilities.

You have to have firm beliefs, otherwise your energy and subconscious actions will sabotage your ability to land and keep customers and clients.

Nine Things You Are Saying and Doing To Make Customers Back Out

There are things that you say, do, feel, or believe that sabotage your sales, even after you've already closed them.

These are innocent things. They are not done on purpose. You might not even realize these things are going on, but it is important to be aware of.

Number 1: Not expecting your sales to stick

This is common. It is the result of having the past experience of customers backing out, so now you expect them to back out. This is a *mindset* aspect of sales, but you have to *expect* to be able to keep the sale in order to actually keep it, otherwise you unintentionally give off vibes that make the customer second guess you and back out.

Hopefully, now that you have the information in this book and you understand what is going on with your customers and yourself, you can change your approach and create a new pattern, where you keep your sales. You have to get rid of the idea that you're not good at sales because it holds you back.

Number 2: Not sticking to your own decisions

This might sound like the Law of Attraction, which you can interpret as attracting clients into your life who are like you. If you are a person who does not stick to your decisions, then the people who you attract are ones who tend not to stick to their decisions, because it is a perfect match.

That is why we should always be the type of client we want to have.

If you're giving a vendor, associate, or anyone else the runaround, stop it! You're just attracting that to yourself.

Number 3: Not using the services or practices that you endorse

If you're a business coach that doesn't have a coach or if you're an accountant, but you can't keep your financial records straight, it shines through. You don't have to admit it to the prospect. People tend to know when you're living what you're teaching.

Living it gives you perspective that you naturally speak from and wisdom that you share that isn't scripted, it just comes out. Besides, no one likes a hypocrite, so do your best to live in accordance with what you sell and/or teach. That doesn't mean you have to be perfect, but you do have to be able to demonstrate where the principles you are asking people to invest in are working for you in your own life and that it's definitely worth the money.

Number 4: Not knowing the details of why the prospect wants or needs your help

How can you sell something to somebody when you don't know what they're looking for? You don't know what *they* think they need; you don't know why they are talking to you. You hear what they're saying, but you feel like every prospect is saying the same thing, so you don't really see *them*.

That doesn't work. You need to know the details of why they are talking to you, so that you can respond intelligently – this includes emotional intelligence. You need to have a full understanding of their situation, which includes knowing what they need to know to feel comfortable making a decision to buy.

Don't lump all prospects together. See the individual and they will see *you!*

Number 5: Not being prepared with responses to their concerns

The majority of sales trainers call a prospect's concerns "objections" and your responses to them "rebuttals." I don't like those terms, because I feel like it sounds confrontational, or like a debate, and I'm not going to debate with anyone about buying. I will, however, respond to a concern. This is the right thing to do, especially in staying in integrity with wanting my potential client to be able to benefit from the product or service the way I know they can. I tell them what they need to know to make them feel better about taking the risk because it's the caring and compassionate thing to do.

When you are organized, you have responses to the most common concerns you hear, but you're sabotaging the interaction and ultimately the sale, when you look at their concerns as "objections" and your responses as "rebuttals" and even the fact that they have concerns as "conflict". Do not treat it as a situation where you must "win them over." Your objective should be more meaningful than that.

Number 6: Not starting immediately when they say yes

We're going to talk more about this in the next section, but for now, you should know that people are more likely to back out when you don't start immediately. Give them something to start working with right away. In some industries, this might take some creativity, but information and "homework assignments" can always be created for this.

Number 7: You didn't address their fears and "what-ifs" about working together

The entire training is about this. Sometimes, even when you ask a person, "Do you have any questions or concerns about getting this service from me?" they will say "No." It is because *they* don't realize their concerns themselves.

This is why you must be systematic in asking the right questions, addressing common issues and concerns you are aware of, having your guarantee, etc. If they are afraid of buying from you, you will not be able to make or keep the sale, period.

Number 8: You let them believe they're making a purchase instead of making an investment

This is a big deal. A purchase equals spending money. Money is gone after a purchase. An investment, on the other hand, is an opportunity to *gain* money or to gain something that will be equivalent to money; something of value. Money is potentially on its way back to you the second you make an investment.

I'm talking about losing vs. gaining. You must make it known that the person is being given the opportunity to multiply, not to subtract. If you can't figure out how your product can serve as an investment for your customer, that is your homework assignment!

Number 9: You let them believe that the things they give up in order to be able to invest in your services are sacrifices instead of offerings

It is a huge mindset shift to switch from thinking in terms of sacrificing to thinking in terms of offerings.

The psychology behind it is simple. Whatever people give up that they would rather not give up is seen as a sacrifice. A sacrifice is generally something you don't want to do, which means a sacrifice usually has a negative connotation. But an offering has a positive connotation. Offerings are given gladly and freely, because the giver has faith. Offerings are given out of love – love for oneself and love for the cause – and in church they are called *love offerings*.

You want people to think of what they had to give up to begin working with you as an offering instead of a sacrifice. This way of thinking results in less resistance and more trust.

They are not giving an offering to you or for you. If anything, it is for them, but more powerful than that is the fact that they are placing an offering to show their belief in the concept of abundance, reciprocity, and knowing they will receive remarkable returns as a result of buying from you.

And More...

There could be a host of other things you are saying and doing to make your clients back out. I only gave you nine common ones to start with.

While it might sound crazy, I don't advise you to try to be a perfect salesperson. Perfection is unrealistic. Aim, instead, to master a few of the things on this list. Then master a few more and keep expanding your mastery until you are highly proficient in retaining sales.

If you are present, thorough, authentic, and trustworthy, things will work in your favor.

A Shrewd and Selfless Way to Make Your Sales Stick

The goal of any sales book is to help you get your customer to agree to buy something. The goal of this book is not only for that to happen, but to ensure they never back out of the sale.

Let's assume you got them to say yes. What is one last thing you can do to ensure they never back out? There is a strategy, but you must act fast!

The moment your customer says "Yes," send them something valuable. Email them a "good faith gift." If you are a coach or consultant, e-mail them a gift that has special content or information regarding whatever it is that you're teaching or selling. Send them a video or an audio or an e-book or a chart that they can begin studying right now. You can do it while they're still on the phone.

In addition to sending out the New Client Information form and the Letter of Agreement (contract), you should have a welcome package you send immediately, which helps the client stay enthused and engaged, and verifies that they made the right decision to do business with you. They are getting immediate value and are too busy using the materials you sent to think about backing out and returning anything.

This strategy also allows them to say to the naysayers – people who feel they shouldn't being doing this – that it's too late. "I've already started!"

Your good faith gift reduces the chances of them backing out because if they have any kind of conscience, they won't want you to think they are stealing from you by taking your gift then backing out. You did something in good faith, so they'll return the gesture.

The Limitations of This Training vs. My Free Gift

There are many things this training doesn't address, some of which I have already mentioned. You might notice that I didn't teach how to properly use urgency in your marketing so that customers buy *now* instead of waiting until later. I didn't teach about how to get testimonials if you haven't actually closed a sale yet. I didn't discuss the mechanics of how to formulate a powerful guarantee. I didn't teach about websites, auto-responders, blogging, branding, referrals, joint ventures, speaking engagements, and a host of other topics related to marketing and sales, online and offline.

When you work with me, we address these things if and when the need arises, based on where you are in your business. As a valued reader, I am offering you the opportunity to receive a complimentary "Keeping the Sale" coaching session with me, by sending an email request to my assistant at freesessions@georgiabusinesswomen.com. We can explore some of the areas this book doesn't address and discuss how you can move forward.

Please allow one hour for the session, which will occur on a Wednesday or Friday. Other questions, concerns, or feedback can be directed to inquiries@georgiabusinesswomen.com.

Gratitude

Thank you again for reading this book! It gives me great pleasure to be able to share my passion for business with the world.

If reading this book has been a help to you, please leave an online review so that other people might be encouraged to read this book too.

It only takes a few minutes, because it doesn't have to be perfect, it just has to be real!

Wishing you many blessings so that you can continue to bless others!

-Freedom Claudine Hunt aka Yaa Diaspora
The Power Woman's Confidante

Insights and Notes